books by
BOXER

www.booksbyboxer.com

Published by
Books By Boxer, Leeds, LS13 4BS UK
Books by Boxer (EU), Dublin D02 P593 IRELAND
© Books By Boxer 2022
All Rights Reserved
MADE IN CHINA
ISBN: 9781909732810

No part of this publication may be reproduced or transmitted in any form or by any means, electronic or mechanical, including photocopying, recording or any information storage and retrieval system, or for the source of ideas without written permission from the publisher.

THIS Beer BIBLE BELONGS TO:

IF FOUND, PLEASE CALL:

LOCATION:

DATE:

BEER NAME: **BEER STYLE:** **BREWERY:**

COLOUR:

CLARITY:

CLOUDY ☐☐☐☐☐☐☐☐☐☐ CRYSTAL

HEAD:

HEADLESS ☐☐☐☐☐☐☐☐☐☐ FLAKE?

HOP SCALE:

TASTE:

hoppy / malty / sweet / roasty / sour / other _____

AROMA:

hoppy / malty / fruity / floral / sour / other _____

NOTES: _____

AFTER TASTE: /10

DRINKABILITY: /10

DON'T DRINK AGAIN: 🍺 MIGHT ORDER AGAIN: 🍺 GOING TO ORDER ANOTHER: 🍺

LOCATION: **DATE:**

BEER NAME: **BEER STYLE:** **BREWERY:**

COLOUR:

CLARITY:
CLOUDY ▭▭▭▭▭▭▭▭▭▭ CRYSTAL

HEAD:
HEADLESS ▭▭▭▭▭▭▭▭▭▭ FLAKE?

HOP SCALE:

TASTE:
hoppy / malty / sweet / roasty / sour / other _____

AROMA:
hoppy / malty / fruity / floral / sour / other _____

NOTES: _____

AFTER TASTE: /10

DRINKABILITY: /10

DON'T DRINK AGAIN: **MIGHT ORDER AGAIN:** **GOING TO ORDER ANOTHER:**

LOCATION:

DATE:

BEER NAME: **BEER STYLE:** **BREWERY:**

COLOUR:

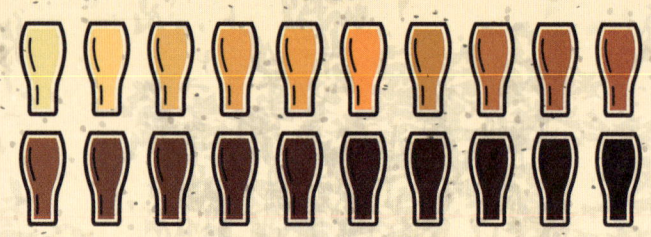

CLARITY:
CLOUDY ☐☐☐☐☐☐☐☐☐☐ CRYSTAL

HEAD:
HEADLESS ☐☐☐☐☐☐☐☐☐☐ FLAKE?

HOP SCALE:

TASTE:
hoppy / malty / sweet / roasty / sour / other _____

AROMA:
hoppy / malty / fruity / floral / sour / other _____

NOTES: _____

AFTER TASTE: /10

DRINKABILITY: /10

DON'T DRINK AGAIN: 🍺   MIGHT ORDER AGAIN: 🍺   GOING TO ORDER ANOTHER: 🍺

LOCATION:

DATE:

BEER NAME: **BEER STYLE:** **BREWERY:**

COLOUR:

CLARITY:

CLOUDY ☐☐☐☐☐☐☐☐☐☐ CRYSTAL

HEAD:

HEADLESS ☐☐☐☐☐☐☐☐☐☐ FLAKE?

HOP SCALE:

TASTE:

hoppy / malty / sweet / roasty / sour / other _____

AROMA:

hoppy / malty / fruity / floral / sour / other _____

NOTES: _____

AFTER TASTE: /10

DRINKABILITY: /10

DON'T DRINK AGAIN: **MIGHT ORDER AGAIN:** **GOING TO ORDER ANOTHER:**

LOCATION:

DATE:

BEER NAME: **BEER STYLE:** **BREWERY:**

COLOUR:

CLARITY:

CLOUDY ▭▭▭▭▭▭▭▭▭▭ CRYSTAL

HEAD:

HEADLESS ▭▭▭▭▭▭▭▭▭▭ FLAKE?

HOP SCALE:

TASTE:
hoppy / malty / sweet / roasty / sour / other _____

AROMA:
hoppy / malty / fruity / floral / sour / other _____

NOTES: _____

AFTER TASTE: /10

DRINKABILITY: /10

DON'T DRINK AGAIN: MIGHT ORDER AGAIN: GOING TO ORDER ANOTHER:

LOCATION: **DATE:**

BEER NAME: **BEER STYLE:**   **BREWERY:**

COLOUR:

CLARITY:
CLOUDY ☐☐☐☐☐☐☐☐☐☐ CRYSTAL

HEAD:
HEADLESS ☐☐☐☐☐☐☐☐☐☐ FLAKE?

HOP SCALE:

TASTE:
hoppy / malty / sweet / roasty / sour / other _____

AROMA:
hoppy / malty / fruity / floral / sour / other _____

NOTES: _____

AFTER TASTE: /10

DRINKABILITY: /10

DON'T DRINK AGAIN: 🌰   **MIGHT ORDER AGAIN:** 🌰   **GOING TO ORDER ANOTHER:** 🌰

BEER TRIVIA
Quiz

1. WHICH OF THE FOLLOWING IS NOT A TYPE OF HOP?
A) Pilgrim **B)** Tomahawk **C)** Captain **D)** Admiral

2. CLAIMED TO BE THE STRONGEST BEER IN THE WORLD, HOW MUCH ALCOHOL PERCENT (ABV) DOES BREWMEISTER'S SNAKE VENOM HAVE?
A) 62.5% **B)** 70% **C)** 65% **D)** 67.5%

3. WHICH COUNTRY CONSUMES THE MOST BEER PER CAPITA ANNUALLY?
A) Germany **B)** Czech Republic **C)** Poland **D)** Ireland

4. WHERE WAS PILSNER INVENTED?
A) USA **B)** UK **C)** Belgium **D)** Czech Republic

5. WHICH COUNTRY DID THE GREAT BEER FLOOD OCCUR IN 1814, WHERE MORE THAN 320,000 GALLONS OF BEER BURST OUT INTO THE STREET?
A) United Kingdom **B)** Germany **C)** Ireland **D)** USA

ANSWERS: 1. C, 2. D, 3. B, 4. D, 5. A

LOCATION: **DATE:**

BEER NAME: **BEER STYLE:** **BREWERY:**

COLOUR:

CLARITY:
CLOUDY ☐☐☐☐☐☐☐☐☐☐ CRYSTAL

HEAD:
HEADLESS ☐☐☐☐☐☐☐☐☐☐ FLAKE?

HOP SCALE:

TASTE:
hoppy / malty / sweet / roasty / sour / other _____

AROMA:
hoppy / malty / fruity / floral / sour / other _____

NOTES: _____

AFTER TASTE: /10

DRINKABILITY: /10

DON'T DRINK AGAIN: ⬡   **MIGHT ORDER AGAIN:** ⬡   **GOING TO ORDER ANOTHER:** ⬡

LOCATION:

DATE:

BEER NAME: **BEER STYLE:**   **BREWERY:**

COLOUR:

CLARITY:
CLOUDY ☐☐☐☐☐☐☐☐☐☐ CRYSTAL

HEAD:
HEADLESS ☐☐☐☐☐☐☐☐☐☐ FLAKE?

HOP SCALE:

TASTE:
hoppy / malty / sweet / roasty / sour / other _____

AROMA:
hoppy / malty / fruity / floral / sour / other _____

NOTES: _____

AFTER TASTE: /10

DRINKABILITY: /10

DON'T DRINK AGAIN: **MIGHT ORDER AGAIN:**   **GOING TO ORDER ANOTHER:**

LOCATION: **DATE:**

BEER NAME: **BEER STYLE:** **BREWERY:**

COLOUR:

CLARITY:
CLOUDY ☐☐☐☐☐☐☐☐☐☐ CRYSTAL

HEAD:
HEADLESS ☐☐☐☐☐☐☐☐☐☐ FLAKE?

HOP SCALE:

TASTE:
hoppy / malty / sweet / roasty / sour / other _____

AROMA:
hoppy / malty / fruity / floral / sour / other _____

NOTES: _____

AFTER TASTE: /10

DRINKABILITY: /10

DON'T DRINK AGAIN: **MIGHT ORDER AGAIN:** **GOING TO ORDER ANOTHER:**

LOCATION:

DATE:

BEER NAME: **BEER STYLE:** **BREWERY:**

COLOUR:

CLARITY:

CLOUDY ☐☐☐☐☐☐☐☐☐☐ CRYSTAL

HEAD:

HEADLESS ☐☐☐☐☐☐☐☐☐☐ FLAKE?

HOP SCALE:

TASTE:
hoppy / malty / sweet / roasty / sour / other _____

AROMA:
hoppy / malty / fruity / floral / sour / other _____

NOTES: _____

AFTER TASTE: /10

DRINKABILITY: /10

DON'T DRINK AGAIN: **MIGHT ORDER AGAIN:** **GOING TO ORDER ANOTHER:**

LOCATION:

DATE:

BEER NAME: **BEER STYLE:** **BREWERY:**

COLOUR:

CLARITY:
CLOUDY ▢▢▢▢▢▢▢▢▢▢ CRYSTAL

HEAD:
HEADLESS ▢▢▢▢▢▢▢▢▢▢ FLAKE?

HOP SCALE:

TASTE:
hoppy / malty / sweet / roasty / sour / other _____

AROMA:
hoppy / malty / fruity / floral / sour / other _____

NOTES: _____

AFTER TASTE: /10

DRINKABILITY: /10

DON'T DRINK AGAIN: 🌿 MIGHT ORDER AGAIN: 🌿 GOING TO ORDER ANOTHER: 🌿

LOCATION:

DATE:

BEER NAME: **BEER STYLE:**   **BREWERY:**

COLOUR:

CLARITY:

CLOUDY ☐☐☐☐☐☐☐☐☐☐ CRYSTAL

HEAD:

HEADLESS ☐☐☐☐☐☐☐☐☐☐ FLAKE?

HOP SCALE:

TASTE:

hoppy / malty / sweet / roasty / sour / other _____

AROMA:

hoppy / malty / fruity / floral / sour / other _____

NOTES: _____

AFTER TASTE: /10

DRINKABILITY: /10

DON'T DRINK AGAIN: 🌰   MIGHT ORDER AGAIN: 🌰   GOING TO ORDER ANOTHER: 🌰

LOCATION:

DATE:

BEER NAME:

BEER STYLE:

BREWERY:

COLOUR:

CLARITY:
CLOUDY ▭▭▭▭▭▭▭▭▭▭ CRYSTAL

HEAD:
HEADLESS ▭▭▭▭▭▭▭▭▭▭ FLAKE?

HOP SCALE:

TASTE:
hoppy / malty / sweet / roasty / sour / other _____

AROMA:
hoppy / malty / fruity / floral / sour / other _____

NOTES: _____

AFTER TASTE: /10

DRINKABILITY: /10

DON'T DRINK AGAIN: 　 MIGHT ORDER AGAIN: 　 GOING TO ORDER ANOTHER:

CENOSILLICAPHOBIA

(Pronounced sen-no-sill-ick-uh-fobia)

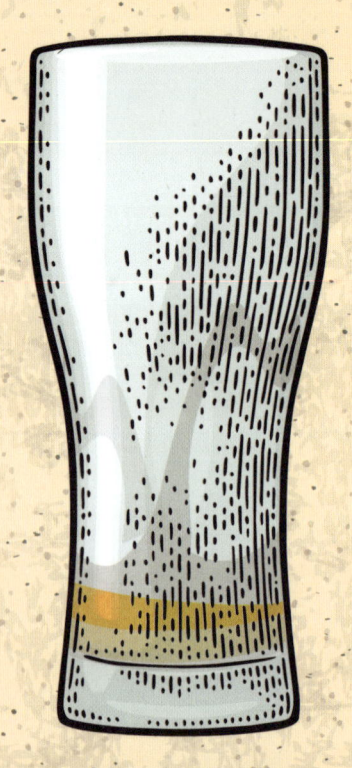

IS THE FEAR OF AN EMPTY GLASS

LOCATION: **DATE:**

BEER NAME: **BEER STYLE:** **BREWERY:**

COLOUR:

CLARITY:
CLOUDY ☐☐☐☐☐☐☐☐☐ CRYSTAL

HEAD:
HEADLESS ☐☐☐☐☐☐☐☐☐ FLAKE?

HOP SCALE:

TASTE:
hoppy / malty / sweet / roasty / sour / other _____

AROMA:
hoppy / malty / fruity / floral / sour / other _____

NOTES: _____

AFTER TASTE: /10

DRINKABILITY: /10

DON'T DRINK AGAIN: **MIGHT ORDER AGAIN:** **GOING TO ORDER ANOTHER:**

LOCATION: **DATE:**

BEER NAME: **BEER STYLE:** **BREWERY:**

COLOUR:

CLARITY:
CLOUDY ▢▢▢▢▢▢▢▢▢▢ CRYSTAL

HEAD:
HEADLESS ▢▢▢▢▢▢▢▢▢▢ FLAKE?

HOP SCALE:

TASTE:
hoppy / malty / sweet / roasty / sour / other _____

AROMA:
hoppy / malty / fruity / floral / sour / other _____

NOTES: _____ **AFTER TASTE:** /10

_____ **DRINKABILITY:** /10

DON'T DRINK AGAIN: **MIGHT ORDER AGAIN:** **GOING TO ORDER ANOTHER:**

LOCATION: **DATE:**

BEER NAME: **BEER STYLE:** **BREWERY:**

COLOUR:

CLARITY:
CLOUDY ☐☐☐☐☐☐☐☐☐☐ CRYSTAL

HEAD:
HEADLESS ☐☐☐☐☐☐☐☐☐☐ FLAKE?

HOP SCALE:

TASTE:
hoppy / malty / sweet / roasty / sour / other _____

AROMA:
hoppy / malty / fruity / floral / sour / other _____

NOTES: _____

AFTER TASTE: /10

DRINKABILITY: /10

DON'T DRINK AGAIN: 🌰 **MIGHT ORDER AGAIN:** 🌰 **GOING TO ORDER ANOTHER:** 🌰

LOCATION: **DATE:**

BEER NAME: **BEER STYLE:** **BREWERY:**

COLOUR:

CLARITY:
CLOUDY ☐☐☐☐☐☐☐☐☐☐ CRYSTAL

HEAD:
HEADLESS ☐☐☐☐☐☐☐☐☐☐ FLAKE?

HOP SCALE:

TASTE:
hoppy / malty / sweet / roasty / sour / other _____

AROMA:
hoppy / malty / fruity / floral / sour / other _____

NOTES: _____

AFTER TASTE: /10

DRINKABILITY: /10

DON'T DRINK AGAIN: 🌿 MIGHT ORDER AGAIN: 🌿 GOING TO ORDER ANOTHER: 🌿

LOCATION:

DATE:

BEER NAME: **BEER STYLE:** **BREWERY:**

COLOUR:

CLARITY:

CLOUDY ☐☐☐☐☐☐☐☐☐☐ CRYSTAL

HEAD:

HEADLESS ☐☐☐☐☐☐☐☐☐☐ FLAKE?

HOP SCALE:

TASTE:
hoppy / malty / sweet / roasty / sour / other _____

AROMA:
hoppy / malty / fruity / floral / sour / other _____

NOTES: _____

AFTER TASTE: /10

DRINKABILITY: /10

DON'T DRINK AGAIN: **MIGHT ORDER AGAIN:** **GOING TO ORDER ANOTHER:**

LOCATION:

DATE:

BEER NAME: **BEER STYLE:** **BREWERY:**

COLOUR:

CLARITY:

CLOUDY ☐☐☐☐☐☐☐☐☐☐ CRYSTAL

HEAD:

HEADLESS ☐☐☐☐☐☐☐☐☐☐ FLAKE?

HOP SCALE:

TASTE:

hoppy / malty / sweet / roasty / sour / other _____

AROMA:

hoppy / malty / fruity / floral / sour / other _____

NOTES: _____

AFTER TASTE: /10

DRINKABILITY: /10

DON'T DRINK AGAIN: 🍺 MIGHT ORDER AGAIN: 🍺 GOING TO ORDER ANOTHER: 🍺

LOCATION: **DATE:**

BEER NAME: **BEER STYLE:**   **BREWERY:**

COLOUR:

CLARITY:

CLOUDY ▭▭▭▭▭▭▭▭▭▭ CRYSTAL

HEAD:

HEADLESS ▭▭▭▭▭▭▭▭▭▭ FLAKE?

HOP SCALE:

TASTE:
hoppy / malty / sweet / roasty / sour / other _____

AROMA:
hoppy / malty / fruity / floral / sour / other _____

NOTES: _____

AFTER TASTE: /10

DRINKABILITY: /10

DON'T DRINK AGAIN: 🌿   MIGHT ORDER AGAIN: 🌿   GOING TO ORDER ANOTHER: 🌿

to me
'DRINK RESPONSIBLY'
means
DON'T SPILL IT!

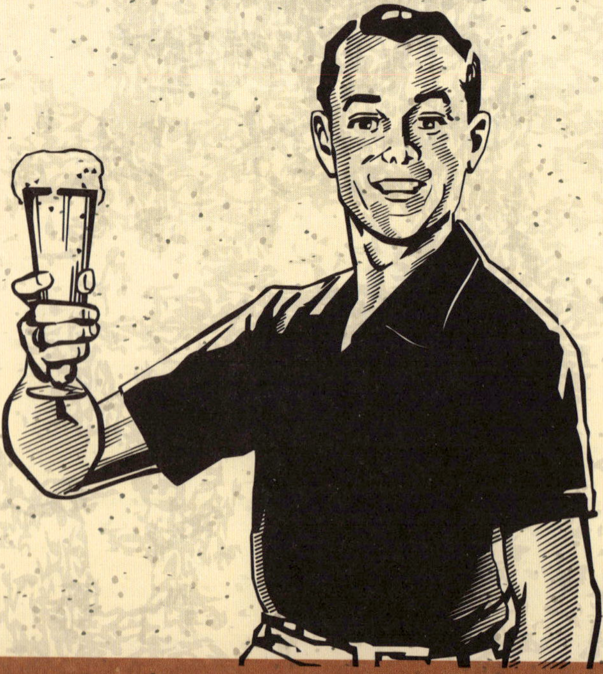

LOCATION: **DATE:**

BEER NAME: **BEER STYLE:** **BREWERY:**

COLOUR:

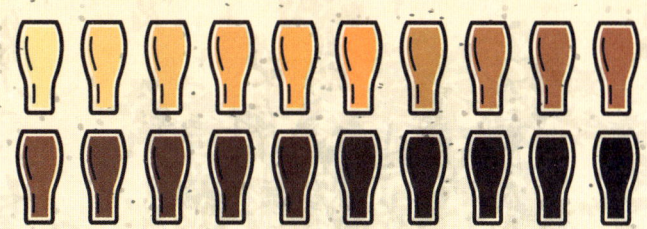

CLARITY:
CLOUDY ▭▭▭▭▭▭▭▭▭▭ CRYSTAL

HEAD:
HEADLESS ▭▭▭▭▭▭▭▭▭▭ FLAKE?

HOP SCALE:

TASTE:
hoppy / malty / sweet / roasty / sour / other _____

AROMA:
hoppy / malty / fruity / floral / sour / other _____

NOTES: _____

AFTER TASTE: /10

DRINKABILITY: /10

DON'T DRINK AGAIN: ⬡ **MIGHT ORDER AGAIN:** ⬡ **GOING TO ORDER ANOTHER:** ⬡

LOCATION: **DATE:**

BEER NAME: **BEER STYLE:**   **BREWERY:**

COLOUR:

CLARITY:
CLOUDY ▭▭▭▭▭▭▭▭▭▭ CRYSTAL

HEAD:
HEADLESS ▭▭▭▭▭▭▭▭▭▭ FLAKE?

HOP SCALE:

TASTE:
hoppy / malty / sweet / roasty / sour / other _____

AROMA:
hoppy / malty / fruity / floral / sour / other _____

NOTES: _____   **AFTER TASTE:** /10

_____

_____   **DRINKABILITY:** /10

DON'T DRINK AGAIN   **MIGHT ORDER AGAIN**   **GOING TO ORDER ANOTHER**

LOCATION:

BEER NAME: **BEER STYLE:** **BREWERY:**

DATE:

COLOUR:

CLARITY:
CLOUDY ☐☐☐☐☐☐☐☐☐ CRYSTAL

HEAD:
HEADLESS ☐☐☐☐☐☐☐☐☐ FLAKE?

HOP SCALE:

TASTE:
hoppy / malty / sweet / roasty / sour / other _____

AROMA:
hoppy / malty / fruity / floral / sour / other _____

NOTES: _____
_____
_____

AFTER TASTE: /10

DRINKABILITY: /10

DON'T DRINK AGAIN: 🌰 MIGHT ORDER AGAIN: 🌰 GOING TO ORDER ANOTHER: 🌰

LOCATION:

DATE:

BEER NAME: **BEER STYLE:** **BREWERY:**

COLOUR:

CLARITY:
CLOUDY ☐☐☐☐☐☐☐☐☐☐ CRYSTAL

HEAD:
HEADLESS ☐☐☐☐☐☐☐☐☐☐ FLAKE?

HOP SCALE:

TASTE:
hoppy / malty / sweet / roasty / sour / other _____

AROMA:
hoppy / malty / fruity / floral / sour / other _____

NOTES: _____

AFTER TASTE: /10

DRINKABILITY: /10

DON'T DRINK AGAIN: ☁ **MIGHT ORDER AGAIN:** ☁ **GOING TO ORDER ANOTHER:** ☁

LOCATION: **DATE:**

BEER NAME: **BEER STYLE:** **BREWERY:**

COLOUR:

CLARITY:
CLOUDY ☐☐☐☐☐☐☐☐☐☐ CRYSTAL

HEAD:
HEADLESS ☐☐☐☐☐☐☐☐☐☐ FLAKE?

HOP SCALE:

TASTE:
hoppy / malty / sweet / roasty / sour / other _____

AROMA:
hoppy / malty / fruity / floral / sour / other _____

NOTES: _____
_____
_____

AFTER TASTE: /10

DRINKABILITY: /10

DON'T DRINK AGAIN: 🌿 MIGHT ORDER AGAIN: 🌿 GOING TO ORDER ANOTHER: 🌿

LOCATION:

DATE:

BEER NAME: **BEER STYLE:** **BREWERY:**

COLOUR:

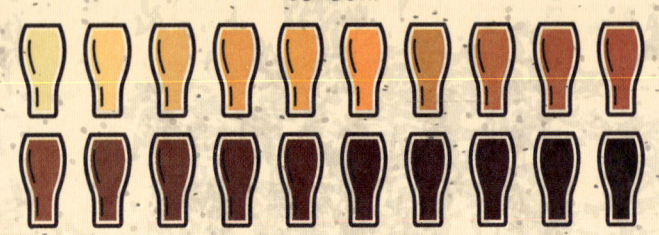

CLARITY:

CLOUDY ☐☐☐☐☐☐☐☐☐ CRYSTAL

HEAD:

HEADLESS ☐☐☐☐☐☐☐☐☐ FLAKE?

HOP SCALE:

TASTE:
hoppy / malty / sweet / roasty / sour / other _____

AROMA:
hoppy / malty / fruity / floral / sour / other _____

NOTES: _____

AFTER TASTE: /10

DRINKABILITY: /10

DON'T DRINK AGAIN: 🌰   MIGHT ORDER AGAIN: 🌰   GOING TO ORDER ANOTHER: 🌰

LOCATION:

DATE:

BEER NAME: **BEER STYLE:**   **BREWERY:**

COLOUR:

CLARITY:
CLOUDY ☐☐☐☐☐☐☐☐☐☐ CRYSTAL

HEAD:
HEADLESS ☐☐☐☐☐☐☐☐☐☐ FLAKE?

HOP SCALE:

TASTE:
hoppy / malty / sweet / roasty / sour / other _____

AROMA:
hoppy / malty / fruity / floral / sour / other _____

NOTES: _____

AFTER TASTE: /10

DRINKABILITY: /10

DON'T DRINK AGAIN: 🌰 **MIGHT ORDER AGAIN:** 🌰 **GOING TO ORDER ANOTHER:** 🌰

IN MEDIEVAL EUROPE, AS BEER HAD
UNDERGONE FERMENTATION, IT WAS CLEANER
AND SAFER TO DRINK THAN WATER. THIS LED
TO OVER 220-250 LITRES OF BEER BEING
CONSUMED A YEAR BY THE AVERAGE PERSON!

CHILDREN WERE ALSO ENCOURAGED TO DRINK
BEER FOR NUTRITIONAL BENEFITS.

WHILST IN THE 1600S, MIDWIVES CREATED
SUPER-STRONG BEER TO EASE THE PAIN
OF LABOUR!

LOCATION:

DATE:

BEER NAME: **BEER STYLE:** **BREWERY:**

COLOUR:

CLARITY:

CLOUDY ☐☐☐☐☐☐☐☐☐☐ CRYSTAL

HEAD:

HEADLESS ☐☐☐☐☐☐☐☐☐☐ FLAKE?

HOP SCALE:

TASTE:
hoppy / malty / sweet / roasty / sour / other _____

AROMA:
hoppy / malty / fruity / floral / sour / other _____

NOTES: _____

AFTER TASTE: /10

DRINKABILITY: /10

DON'T DRINK AGAIN: ❀ MIGHT ORDER AGAIN: ❀ GOING TO ORDER ANOTHER: ❀

LOCATION: **DATE:**

BEER NAME: **BEER STYLE:** **BREWERY:**

COLOUR:

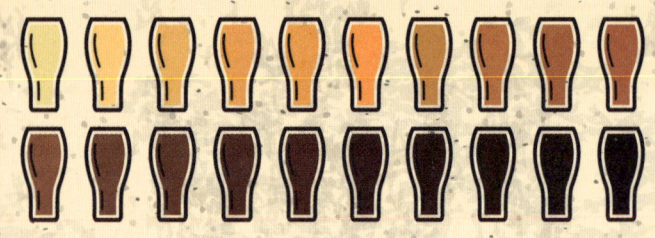

CLARITY:
CLOUDY ▭▭▭▭▭▭▭▭▭ CRYSTAL

HEAD:
HEADLESS ▭▭▭▭▭▭▭▭▭ FLAKE?

HOP SCALE:

TASTE:
hoppy / malty / sweet / roasty / sour / other _____

AROMA:
hoppy / malty / fruity / floral / sour / other _____

NOTES: _____

AFTER TASTE: /10

DRINKABILITY: /10

DON'T DRINK AGAIN: 🍺 MIGHT ORDER AGAIN: 🍺 GOING TO ORDER ANOTHER: 🍺

LOCATION:

DATE:

BEER NAME: **BEER STYLE:** **BREWERY:**

COLOUR:

CLARITY:

CLOUDY ▭▭▭▭▭▭▭▭▭▭ CRYSTAL

HEAD:

HEADLESS ▭▭▭▭▭▭▭▭▭▭ FLAKE?

HOP SCALE:

TASTE:

hoppy / malty / sweet / roasty / sour / other _____

AROMA:

hoppy / malty / fruity / floral / sour / other _____

NOTES: _____

AFTER TASTE: /10

DRINKABILITY: /10

DON'T DRINK AGAIN: 🌰 **MIGHT ORDER AGAIN:** 🌰 **GOING TO ORDER ANOTHER:** 🌰

LOCATION: **DATE:**

BEER NAME: **BEER STYLE:**   **BREWERY:**

COLOUR:

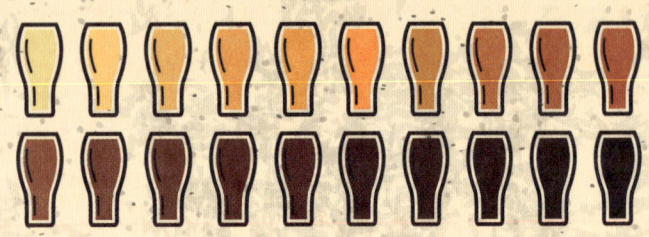

CLARITY:
CLOUDY ☐☐☐☐☐☐☐☐☐☐ CRYSTAL

HEAD:
HEADLESS ☐☐☐☐☐☐☐☐☐☐ FLAKE?

HOP SCALE:

TASTE:
hoppy / malty / sweet / roasty / sour / other _____

AROMA:
hoppy / malty / fruity / floral / sour / other _____

NOTES: _____

AFTER TASTE: /10

DRINKABILITY: /10

DON'T DRINK AGAIN: ◊   MIGHT ORDER AGAIN: ◊   GOING TO ORDER ANOTHER: ◊

LOCATION:

DATE:

BEER NAME: **BEER STYLE:** **BREWERY:**

COLOUR:

CLARITY:

CLOUDY ▭▭▭▭▭▭▭▭▭▭ CRYSTAL

HEAD:

HEADLESS ▭▭▭▭▭▭▭▭▭▭ FLAKE?

HOP SCALE:

TASTE:
hoppy / malty / sweet / roasty / sour / other _____

AROMA:
hoppy / malty / fruity / floral / sour / other _____

NOTES: _____

AFTER TASTE: /10

DRINKABILITY: /10

DON'T DRINK AGAIN: **MIGHT ORDER AGAIN:**   **GOING TO ORDER ANOTHER:**

LOCATION:

DATE:

BEER NAME: **BEER STYLE:** **BREWERY:**

COLOUR:

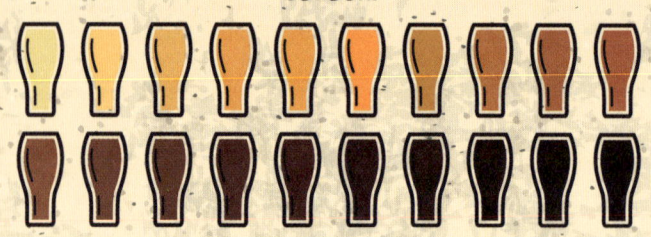

CLARITY:
CLOUDY ☐☐☐☐☐☐☐☐☐☐ CRYSTAL

HEAD:
HEADLESS ☐☐☐☐☐☐☐☐☐☐ FLAKE?

HOP SCALE:

TASTE:
hoppy / malty / sweet / roasty / sour / other _____

AROMA:
hoppy / malty / fruity / floral / sour / other _____

NOTES: _____

AFTER TASTE: /10

DRINKABILITY: /10

DON'T DRINK AGAIN: MIGHT ORDER AGAIN: GOING TO ORDER ANOTHER:

LOCATION: **DATE:**

BEER NAME: **BEER STYLE:** **BREWERY:**

COLOUR:

CLARITY:
CLOUDY ▭▭▭▭▭▭▭▭▭▭ CRYSTAL

HEAD:
HEADLESS ▭▭▭▭▭▭▭▭▭▭ FLAKE?

HOP SCALE:

TASTE:
hoppy / malty / sweet / roasty / sour / other _____

AROMA:
hoppy / malty / fruity / floral / sour / other _____

NOTES: _____

AFTER TASTE: /10

DRINKABILITY: /10

DON'T DRINK AGAIN: **MIGHT ORDER AGAIN:** **GOING TO ORDER ANOTHER:**

Blessed is the Mother Who Gives Birth to a Brewer

—Czech Saying

LOCATION:

DATE:

BEER NAME:　　　**BEER STYLE:**　　　**BREWERY:**

COLOUR:

CLARITY:

CLOUDY　　　　　　　　　　　　　　　　　　　　CRYSTAL

HEAD:

HEADLESS　　　　　　　　　　　　　　　　　　　FLAKE?

HOP SCALE:

TASTE:
hoppy / malty / sweet / roasty / sour / other _____

AROMA:
hoppy / malty / fruity / floral / sour / other _____

NOTES: _____

AFTER TASTE: /10

DRINKABILITY: /10

DON'T DRINK AGAIN:　MIGHT ORDER AGAIN:　GOING TO ORDER ANOTHER:

LOCATION:

DATE:

BEER NAME:　　**BEER STYLE:**　　**BREWERY:**

COLOUR:

CLARITY:

CLOUDY ☐☐☐☐☐☐☐☐☐☐ CRYSTAL

HEAD:

HEADLESS ☐☐☐☐☐☐☐☐☐☐ FLAKE?

HOP SCALE:

TASTE:

hoppy / malty / sweet / roasty / sour / other _____

AROMA:

hoppy / malty / fruity / floral / sour / other _____

NOTES: _____

AFTER TASTE: /10

DRINKABILITY: /10

DON'T DRINK AGAIN　MIGHT ORDER AGAIN　GOING TO ORDER ANOTHER

LOCATION:

DATE:

BEER NAME: **BEER STYLE:** **BREWERY:**

COLOUR:

CLARITY:

CLOUDY ☐☐☐☐☐☐☐☐☐☐ CRYSTAL

HEAD:

HEADLESS ☐☐☐☐☐☐☐☐☐☐ FLAKE?

HOP SCALE:

TASTE:

hoppy / malty / sweet / roasty / sour / other _____

AROMA:

hoppy / malty / fruity / floral / sour / other _____

NOTES: _____

AFTER TASTE: /10

DRINKABILITY: /10

DON'T DRINK AGAIN: **MIGHT ORDER AGAIN:** **GOING TO ORDER ANOTHER:**

LOCATION:

DATE:

BEER NAME: **BEER STYLE:** **BREWERY:**

COLOUR:

CLARITY:

CLOUDY ⬜⬜⬜⬜⬜⬜⬜⬜⬜⬜ CRYSTAL

HEAD:

HEADLESS ⬜⬜⬜⬜⬜⬜⬜⬜⬜⬜ FLAKE?

HOP SCALE:

TASTE:

hoppy / malty / sweet / roasty / sour / other _____

AROMA:

hoppy / malty / fruity / floral / sour / other _____

NOTES: _____

AFTER TASTE: /10

DRINKABILITY: /10

DON'T DRINK AGAIN: 　MIGHT ORDER AGAIN: 　GOING TO ORDER ANOTHER:

LOCATION: **DATE:**

BEER NAME: **BEER STYLE:** **BREWERY:**

COLOUR:

CLARITY:
CLOUDY ☐☐☐☐☐☐☐☐☐☐ CRYSTAL

HEAD:
HEADLESS ☐☐☐☐☐☐☐☐☐☐ FLAKE?

HOP SCALE:

TASTE:
hoppy / malty / sweet / roasty / sour / other _____

AROMA:
hoppy / malty / fruity / floral / sour / other _____

NOTES: _____
_____
_____

AFTER TASTE: /10

DRINKABILITY: /10

DON'T DRINK AGAIN: 🌰   MIGHT ORDER AGAIN: 🌰   GOING TO ORDER ANOTHER: 🌰

LOCATION:

DATE:

BEER NAME: **BEER STYLE:** **BREWERY:**

COLOUR:

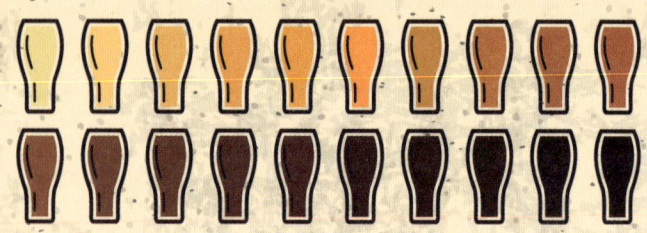

CLARITY:

CLOUDY ☐☐☐☐☐☐☐☐☐☐ CRYSTAL

HEAD:

HEADLESS ☐☐☐☐☐☐☐☐☐☐ FLAKE?

HOP SCALE:

TASTE:

hoppy / malty / sweet / roasty / sour / other _____

AROMA:

hoppy / malty / fruity / floral / sour / other _____

NOTES: _____

AFTER TASTE: /10

DRINKABILITY: /10

DON'T DRINK AGAIN: ☁ MIGHT ORDER AGAIN: ☁ GOING TO ORDER ANOTHER: ☁

LOCATION:

DATE:

BEER NAME: **BEER STYLE:** **BREWERY:**

COLOUR:

CLARITY:

CLOUDY ☐☐☐☐☐☐☐☐☐☐ CRYSTAL

HEAD:

HEADLESS ☐☐☐☐☐☐☐☐☐☐ FLAKE?

HOP SCALE:

TASTE:

hoppy / malty / sweet / roasty / sour / other _____

AROMA:

hoppy / malty / fruity / floral / sour / other _____

NOTES: _____

AFTER TASTE: /10

DRINKABILITY: /10

DON'T DRINK AGAIN: 🍺 **MIGHT ORDER AGAIN:** 🍺 **GOING TO ORDER ANOTHER:** 🍺

"IN A STUDY, SCIENTISTS REPORT THAT DRINKING BEER CAN BE GOOD FOR THE LIVER.

I'm sorry, did I say 'scientists'? I meant Irish people."

— TINA FEY

LOCATION: **DATE:**

BEER NAME: **BEER STYLE:** **BREWERY:**

COLOUR:

CLARITY:
CLOUDY ☐☐☐☐☐☐☐☐☐☐ CRYSTAL

HEAD:
HEADLESS ☐☐☐☐☐☐☐☐☐☐ FLAKE?

HOP SCALE:

TASTE:
hoppy / malty / sweet / roasty / sour / other _____

AROMA:
hoppy / malty / fruity / floral / sour / other _____

NOTES: _____

AFTER TASTE: /10

DRINKABILITY: /10

DON'T DRINK AGAIN: 🌰   MIGHT ORDER AGAIN: 🌰   GOING TO ORDER ANOTHER: 🌰

LOCATION:

DATE:

BEER NAME: **BEER STYLE:** **BREWERY:**

COLOUR:

CLARITY:
CLOUDY ▭▭▭▭▭▭▭▭▭▭ CRYSTAL

HEAD:
HEADLESS ▭▭▭▭▭▭▭▭▭▭ FLAKE?

HOP SCALE:

TASTE:
hoppy / malty / sweet / roasty / sour / other _____

AROMA:
hoppy / malty / fruity / floral / sour / other _____

NOTES: _____

AFTER TASTE: /10

DRINKABILITY: /10

DON'T DRINK AGAIN: ✿   **MIGHT ORDER AGAIN:** ✿   **GOING TO ORDER ANOTHER:** ✿

LOCATION: **DATE:**

BEER NAME: **BEER STYLE:** **BREWERY:**

COLOUR:

CLARITY:

CLOUDY ▢▢▢▢▢▢▢▢▢▢ CRYSTAL

HEAD:

HEADLESS ▢▢▢▢▢▢▢▢▢▢ FLAKE?

HOP SCALE:

TASTE:

hoppy / malty / sweet / roasty / sour / other _____

AROMA:

hoppy / malty / fruity / floral / sour / other _____

NOTES: _____

AFTER TASTE: /10

DRINKABILITY: /10

DON'T DRINK AGAIN: **MIGHT ORDER AGAIN:** **GOING TO ORDER ANOTHER:**

LOCATION: **DATE:**

BEER NAME: **BEER STYLE:** **BREWERY:**

COLOUR:

CLARITY:

CLOUDY ▭▭▭▭▭▭▭▭▭▭ CRYSTAL

HEAD:

HEADLESS ▭▭▭▭▭▭▭▭▭▭ FLAKE?

HOP SCALE:

TASTE:

hoppy / malty / sweet / roasty / sour / other _____

AROMA:

hoppy / malty / fruity / floral / sour / other _____

NOTES: _____

AFTER TASTE: /10

DRINKABILITY: /10

DON'T DRINK AGAIN: **MIGHT ORDER AGAIN:** **GOING TO ORDER ANOTHER:**

LOCATION: **DATE:**

BEER NAME: **BEER STYLE:** **BREWERY:**

COLOUR:

CLARITY:
CLOUDY ▭▭▭▭▭▭▭▭▭▭ CRYSTAL

HEAD:
HEADLESS ▭▭▭▭▭▭▭▭▭▭ FLAKE?

HOP SCALE:

TASTE:
hoppy / malty / sweet / roasty / sour / other _____

AROMA:
hoppy / malty / fruity / floral / sour / other _____

NOTES: _____

AFTER TASTE: /10

DRINKABILITY: /10

DON'T DRINK AGAIN: **MIGHT ORDER AGAIN:** **GOING TO ORDER ANOTHER:**

LOCATION:

DATE:

BEER NAME: **BEER STYLE:** **BREWERY:**

COLOUR:

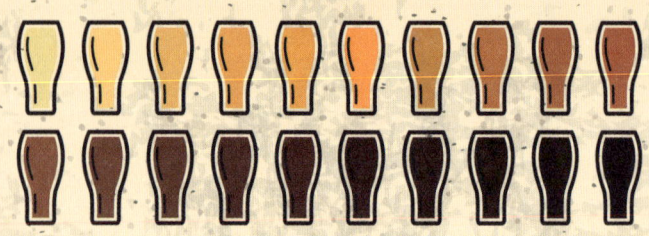

CLARITY:
CLOUDY ☐☐☐☐☐☐☐☐☐☐ CRYSTAL

HEAD:
HEADLESS ☐☐☐☐☐☐☐☐☐☐ FLAKE?

HOP SCALE:

TASTE:
hoppy / malty / sweet / roasty / sour / other _____

AROMA:
hoppy / malty / fruity / floral / sour / other _____

NOTES: _____

AFTER TASTE: /10

DRINKABILITY: /10

DON'T DRINK AGAIN: ☐ **MIGHT ORDER AGAIN:** ☐ **GOING TO ORDER ANOTHER:** ☐

LOCATION: **DATE:**

BEER NAME: **BEER STYLE:** **BREWERY:**

COLOUR:

CLARITY:
CLOUDY ☐☐☐☐☐☐☐☐☐☐ CRYSTAL

HEAD:
HEADLESS ☐☐☐☐☐☐☐☐☐☐ FLAKE?

HOP SCALE:

TASTE:
hoppy / malty / sweet / roasty / sour / other _____

AROMA:
hoppy / malty / fruity / floral / sour / other _____

NOTES: _____

AFTER TASTE: /10

DRINKABILITY: /10

DON'T DRINK AGAIN: 🍺 **MIGHT ORDER AGAIN:** 🍺 **GOING TO ORDER ANOTHER:** 🍺

WHAT ARE Hops?

HOPS ARE A CONE SHAPED FLOWER THAT IS USED IN BREWING BEER. THE PLANTS PRODUCE A FRAGRANT OIL CALLED LUPULIN, WHICH IS WHERE THE HOP'S BITTER, TANGY, FLORAL, AND CITRUS FLAVOURS COME FROM.

THIS CHARACTERISTIC FLAVOUR HELPS DISTINGUISH ONE BEER FROM ANOTHER BY HOW MUCH AND THE VARIETY OF HOP USED.

IN ADDITION TO FLAVOURING, HOPS ALSO HELP TO STABILIZE THE FOAM OF A BEER.

THE UNITED STATES IS THE SECOND LARGEST HOP PRODUCER IN THE WORLD (BEHIND GERMANY).

LOCATION: **DATE:**

BEER NAME: **BEER STYLE:**   **BREWERY:**

COLOUR:

CLARITY:
CLOUDY ☐☐☐☐☐☐☐☐☐☐ CRYSTAL

HEAD:
HEADLESS ☐☐☐☐☐☐☐☐☐☐ FLAKE?

HOP SCALE:

TASTE:
hoppy / malty / sweet / roasty / sour / other _____

AROMA:
hoppy / malty / fruity / floral / sour / other _____

NOTES: _____   **AFTER TASTE:** /10

_____   **DRINKABILITY:** /10

DON'T DRINK AGAIN: ◇   **MIGHT ORDER AGAIN:** ◇   **GOING TO ORDER ANOTHER:** ◇

LOCATION:

DATE:

BEER NAME: **BEER STYLE:**   **BREWERY:**

COLOUR:

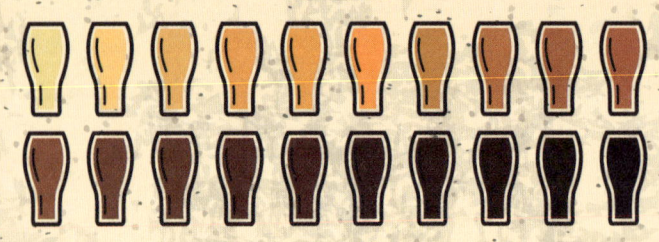

CLARITY:
CLOUDY ☐☐☐☐☐☐☐☐☐☐ CRYSTAL

HEAD:
HEADLESS ☐☐☐☐☐☐☐☐☐☐ FLAKE?

HOP SCALE:

TASTE:
hoppy / malty / sweet / roasty / sour / other _____

AROMA:
hoppy / malty / fruity / floral / sour / other _____

NOTES: _____

AFTER TASTE: /10

DRINKABILITY: /10

DON'T DRINK AGAIN: MIGHT ORDER AGAIN: GOING TO ORDER ANOTHER:

LOCATION: **DATE:**

BEER NAME: **BEER STYLE:** **BREWERY:**

COLOUR:

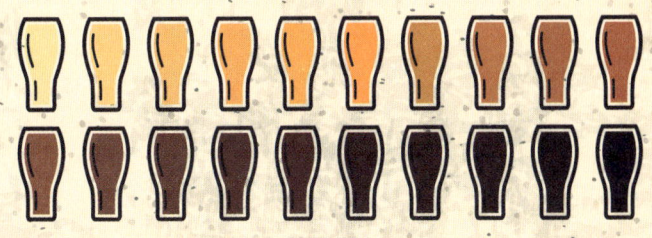

CLARITY:
CLOUDY ▭▭▭▭▭▭▭▭▭▭ CRYSTAL

HEAD:
HEADLESS ▭▭▭▭▭▭▭▭▭▭ FLAKE?

HOP SCALE:

TASTE:
hoppy / malty / sweet / roasty / sour / other _____

AROMA:
hoppy / malty / fruity / floral / sour / other _____

NOTES: _____
_____
_____

AFTER TASTE: /10

DRINKABILITY: /10

DON'T DRINK AGAIN: 🌰 **MIGHT ORDER AGAIN:** 🌰 **GOING TO ORDER ANOTHER:** 🌰

LOCATION:

BEER NAME: **BEER STYLE:** **BREWERY:**

COLOUR:

CLARITY:

CLOUDY ☐☐☐☐☐☐☐☐☐☐ CRYSTAL

HEAD:

HEADLESS ☐☐☐☐☐☐☐☐☐☐ FLAKE?

HOP SCALE:

TASTE:
hoppy / malty / sweet / roasty / sour / other _____

AROMA:
hoppy / malty / fruity / floral / sour / other _____

NOTES: _____

AFTER TASTE: /10

DRINKABILITY: /10

DON'T DRINK AGAIN: ⬠ MIGHT ORDER AGAIN: ⬠ GOING TO ORDER ANOTHER: ⬠

DATE:

LOCATION:

DATE:

BEER NAME: **BEER STYLE:** **BREWERY:**

COLOUR:

CLARITY:

CLOUDY ▭▭▭▭▭▭▭▭▭▭ CRYSTAL

HEAD:

HEADLESS ▭▭▭▭▭▭▭▭▭▭ FLAKE?

HOP SCALE:

TASTE:

hoppy / malty / sweet / roasty / sour / other _____

AROMA:

hoppy / malty / fruity / floral / sour / other _____

NOTES: _____

AFTER TASTE: /10

DRINKABILITY: /10

DON'T DRINK AGAIN: ◯ **MIGHT ORDER AGAIN:** ◯ **GOING TO ORDER ANOTHER:** ◯

LOCATION: **DATE:**

BEER NAME: **BEER STYLE:** **BREWERY:**

COLOUR:

CLARITY:
CLOUDY ☐☐☐☐☐☐☐☐☐☐ CRYSTAL

HEAD:
HEADLESS ☐☐☐☐☐☐☐☐☐☐ FLAKE?

HOP SCALE:

TASTE:
hoppy / malty / sweet / roasty / sour / other _____

AROMA:
hoppy / malty / fruity / floral / sour / other _____

NOTES: _____

AFTER TASTE: /10

DRINKABILITY: /10

DON'T DRINK AGAIN: ☁ **MIGHT ORDER AGAIN:** ☁ **GOING TO ORDER ANOTHER:** ☁

LOCATION:

DATE:

BEER NAME: **BEER STYLE:**   **BREWERY:**

COLOUR:

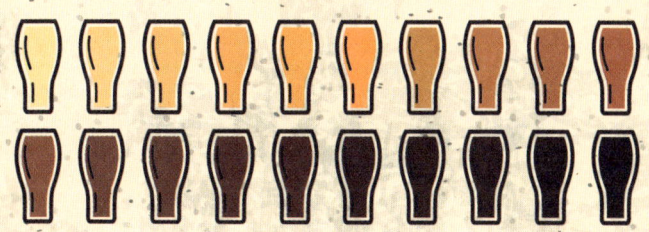

CLARITY:

CLOUDY ▭▭▭▭▭▭▭▭▭▭ CRYSTAL

HEAD:

HEADLESS ▭▭▭▭▭▭▭▭▭▭ FLAKE?

HOP SCALE:

TASTE:

hoppy / malty / sweet / roasty / sour / other _____

AROMA:

hoppy / malty / fruity / floral / sour / other _____

NOTES: _____

AFTER TASTE: /10

DRINKABILITY: /10

DON'T DRINK AGAIN: **MIGHT ORDER AGAIN:**   **GOING TO ORDER ANOTHER:**

MY DOCTOR TOLD ME TO WATCH MY DRINKING...

So I'm off to find a bar with a mirror.

LOCATION: **DATE:**

BEER NAME: **BEER STYLE:** **BREWERY:**

COLOUR:

CLARITY:
CLOUDY ▭▭▭▭▭▭▭▭▭▭ CRYSTAL

HEAD:
HEADLESS ▭▭▭▭▭▭▭▭▭▭ FLAKE?

HOP SCALE:

TASTE:
hoppy / malty / sweet / roasty / sour / other _____

AROMA:
hoppy / malty / fruity / floral / sour / other _____

NOTES: _____

AFTER TASTE: /10

DRINKABILITY: /10

DON'T DRINK AGAIN: **MIGHT ORDER AGAIN:** **GOING TO ORDER ANOTHER:**

LOCATION: **DATE:**

BEER NAME: **BEER STYLE:** **BREWERY:**

COLOUR:

CLARITY:
CLOUDY ▢▢▢▢▢▢▢▢▢▢ CRYSTAL

HEAD:
HEADLESS ▢▢▢▢▢▢▢▢▢▢ FLAKE?

HOP SCALE:

TASTE:
hoppy / malty / sweet / roasty / sour / other _____

AROMA:
hoppy / malty / fruity / floral / sour / other _____

NOTES: _____

AFTER TASTE: /10

DRINKABILITY: /10

DON'T DRINK AGAIN: 🌰 **MIGHT ORDER AGAIN:** 🌰 **GOING TO ORDER ANOTHER:** 🌰

LOCATION: **DATE:**

BEER NAME: **BEER STYLE:** **BREWERY:**

COLOUR:

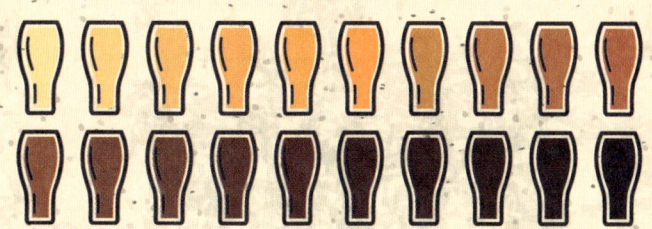

CLARITY:

CLOUDY ☐☐☐☐☐☐☐☐☐☐ CRYSTAL

HEAD:

HEADLESS ☐☐☐☐☐☐☐☐☐☐ FLAKE?

HOP SCALE:

TASTE:
hoppy / malty / sweet / roasty / sour / other _____

AROMA:
hoppy / malty / fruity / floral / sour / other _____

NOTES: _____

AFTER TASTE: /10

DRINKABILITY: /10

DON'T DRINK AGAIN: **MIGHT ORDER AGAIN:** **GOING TO ORDER ANOTHER:**

LOCATION: **DATE:**

BEER NAME: **BEER STYLE:** **BREWERY:**

COLOUR:

CLARITY:
CLOUDY ☐☐☐☐☐☐☐☐☐☐ CRYSTAL

HEAD:
HEADLESS ☐☐☐☐☐☐☐☐☐☐ FLAKE?

HOP SCALE:

TASTE:
hoppy / malty / sweet / roasty / sour / other _____

AROMA:
hoppy / malty / fruity / floral / sour / other _____

NOTES: _____
_____
_____

AFTER TASTE: /10

DRINKABILITY: /10

DON'T DRINK AGAIN: 🍺   MIGHT ORDER AGAIN: 🍺   GOING TO ORDER ANOTHER: 🍺

LOCATION:

DATE:

BEER NAME: **BEER STYLE:** **BREWERY:**

COLOUR:

CLARITY:
CLOUDY ▭▭▭▭▭▭▭▭▭▭ CRYSTAL

HEAD:
HEADLESS ▭▭▭▭▭▭▭▭▭▭ FLAKE?

HOP SCALE:

TASTE:
hoppy / malty / sweet / roasty / sour / other _____

AROMA:
hoppy / malty / fruity / floral / sour / other _____

NOTES: _____

AFTER TASTE: /10

DRINKABILITY: /10

DON'T DRINK AGAIN: **MIGHT ORDER AGAIN:** **GOING TO ORDER ANOTHER:**

LOCATION: **DATE:**

BEER NAME: **BEER STYLE:** **BREWERY:**

COLOUR:

CLARITY:

CLOUDY ▭▭▭▭▭▭▭▭▭▭ CRYSTAL

HEAD:

HEADLESS ▭▭▭▭▭▭▭▭▭▭ FLAKE?

HOP SCALE:

TASTE:
hoppy / malty / sweet / roasty / sour / other _____

AROMA:
hoppy / malty / fruity / floral / sour / other _____

NOTES: _____ **AFTER TASTE:** /10

_____ **DRINKABILITY:** /10

DON'T DRINK AGAIN: **MIGHT ORDER AGAIN:**   **GOING TO ORDER ANOTHER:**

LOCATION:

DATE:

BEER NAME: **BEER STYLE:**   **BREWERY:**

COLOUR:

CLARITY:
CLOUDY ▭▭▭▭▭▭▭▭▭▭ CRYSTAL

HEAD:
HEADLESS ▭▭▭▭▭▭▭▭▭▭ FLAKE?

HOP SCALE:

TASTE:
hoppy / malty / sweet / roasty / sour / other _____

AROMA:
hoppy / malty / fruity / floral / sour / other _____

NOTES: _____

AFTER TASTE: /10

DRINKABILITY: /10

DON'T DRINK AGAIN: **MIGHT ORDER AGAIN:**   **GOING TO ORDER ANOTHER:**

BEER FACTS
TO IMPRESS AT
the Pub

IT IS ALLEGED THAT, THE LONGEST HANGOVER TOOK PLACE AFTER A SCOTSMAN DRANK JUST OVER 28 LITRES OF BEER. IT IS SAID HIS HANGOVER LASTED FOR 4 WEEKS.

VIKINGS BELIEVED THAT WHEN THEY DIED, A GIANT GOAT WOULD BE WAITING FOR THEM. OF COURSE, THIS GOAT'S UDDERS HAD AN UNENDING SUPPLY OF BEER.

IN 2010, THE WORLD'S OLDEST DRINKABLE BEER WAS FOUND ON A BALTIC SEA SHIPWRECK. THE SHIP IS BELIEVED TO HAVE SAILED OVER 200 YEARS AGO.

BEER IS STORED IN DARKER BOTTLES AS EXPOSURE TO LIGHT WILL SPOIL THE BREW.

THE TERM 'RULE OF THUMB' ORIGINATES FROM BREWERS WHO WOULD STICK THEIR THUMB INTO THE MIX TO SEE WHEN THE TEMPERATURE WAS RIGHT FOR ADDING YEAST.

LOCATION:

DATE:

BEER NAME: **BEER STYLE:** **BREWERY:**

COLOUR:

CLARITY:

CLOUDY ☐☐☐☐☐☐☐☐☐☐ CRYSTAL

HEAD:

HEADLESS ☐☐☐☐☐☐☐☐☐☐ FLAKE?

HOP SCALE:

TASTE:

hoppy / malty / sweet / roasty / sour / other _____

AROMA:

hoppy / malty / fruity / floral / sour / other _____

NOTES: _____

AFTER TASTE: /10

DRINKABILITY: /10

DON'T DRINK AGAIN: 🌿 **MIGHT ORDER AGAIN:** 🌿 **GOING TO ORDER ANOTHER:** 🌿

LOCATION:

DATE:

BEER NAME: **BEER STYLE:** **BREWERY:**

COLOUR:

CLARITY:
CLOUDY ☐☐☐☐☐☐☐☐☐☐ CRYSTAL

HEAD:
HEADLESS ☐☐☐☐☐☐☐☐☐☐ FLAKE?

HOP SCALE:

TASTE:
hoppy / malty / sweet / roasty / sour / other _____

AROMA:
hoppy / malty / fruity / floral / sour / other _____

NOTES: _____

AFTER TASTE: /10

DRINKABILITY: /10

DON'T DRINK AGAIN: ○ **MIGHT ORDER AGAIN:** ○ **GOING TO ORDER ANOTHER:** ○

LOCATION: **DATE:**

BEER NAME: **BEER STYLE:** **BREWERY:**

COLOUR:

CLARITY:
CLOUDY ☐☐☐☐☐☐☐☐☐☐ CRYSTAL

HEAD:
HEADLESS ☐☐☐☐☐☐☐☐☐☐ FLAKE?

HOP SCALE:

TASTE:
hoppy / malty / sweet / roasty / sour / other _____

AROMA:
hoppy / malty / fruity / floral / sour / other _____

NOTES: _____

AFTER TASTE: /10

DRINKABILITY: /10

DON'T DRINK AGAIN: ☁ **MIGHT ORDER AGAIN:** ☁ **GOING TO ORDER ANOTHER:** ☁

LOCATION:

DATE:

BEER NAME: **BEER STYLE:**   **BREWERY:**

COLOUR:

CLARITY:
CLOUDY ☐☐☐☐☐☐☐☐☐☐ CRYSTAL

HEAD:
HEADLESS ☐☐☐☐☐☐☐☐☐☐ FLAKE?

HOP SCALE:

TASTE:
hoppy / malty / sweet / roasty / sour / other _____

AROMA:
hoppy / malty / fruity / floral / sour / other _____

NOTES: _____
_____
_____

AFTER TASTE: /10

DRINKABILITY: /10

DON'T DRINK AGAIN: **MIGHT ORDER AGAIN:**   **GOING TO ORDER ANOTHER:**

LOCATION: **DATE:**

BEER NAME: **BEER STYLE:** **BREWERY:**

COLOUR:

CLARITY:
CLOUDY ☐☐☐☐☐☐☐☐☐☐ CRYSTAL

HEAD:
HEADLESS ☐☐☐☐☐☐☐☐☐☐ FLAKE?

HOP SCALE:

TASTE:
hoppy / malty / sweet / roasty / sour / other _____

AROMA:
hoppy / malty / fruity / floral / sour / other _____

NOTES: _____

AFTER TASTE: /10

DRINKABILITY: /10

DON'T DRINK AGAIN: **MIGHT ORDER AGAIN:** **GOING TO ORDER ANOTHER:**

LOCATION: **DATE:**

BEER NAME: **BEER STYLE:** **BREWERY:**

COLOUR:

CLARITY:
CLOUDY ☐☐☐☐☐☐☐☐☐☐ CRYSTAL

HEAD:
HEADLESS ☐☐☐☐☐☐☐☐☐☐ FLAKE?

HOP SCALE:

TASTE:
hoppy / malty / sweet / roasty / sour / other _____

AROMA:
hoppy / malty / fruity / floral / sour / other _____

NOTES: _____
_____
_____

AFTER TASTE: /10

DRINKABILITY: /10

DON'T DRINK AGAIN: 🌰 **MIGHT ORDER AGAIN:** 🌰 **GOING TO ORDER ANOTHER:** 🌰

LOCATION:

DATE:

BEER NAME: **BEER STYLE:** **BREWERY:**

COLOUR:

CLARITY:
CLOUDY ▭▭▭▭▭▭▭▭▭▭ CRYSTAL

HEAD:
HEADLESS ▭▭▭▭▭▭▭▭▭▭ FLAKE?

HOP SCALE:

TASTE:
hoppy / malty / sweet / roasty / sour / other _____

AROMA:
hoppy / malty / fruity / floral / sour / other _____

NOTES: _____

AFTER TASTE: /10

DRINKABILITY: /10

DON'T DRINK AGAIN: **MIGHT ORDER AGAIN:** **GOING TO ORDER ANOTHER:**

"BEER IS PROOF THAT GOD LOVES US AND WANTS US TO BE *Happy.*"

— BENJAMIN FRANKLIN

LOCATION: **DATE:**

BEER NAME: **BEER STYLE:** **BREWERY:**

COLOUR:

CLARITY:
CLOUDY ▢▢▢▢▢▢▢▢▢▢ CRYSTAL

HEAD:
HEADLESS ▢▢▢▢▢▢▢▢▢▢ FLAKE?

HOP SCALE:

TASTE:
hoppy / malty / sweet / roasty / sour / other _____

AROMA:
hoppy / malty / fruity / floral / sour / other _____

NOTES: _____

AFTER TASTE: /10

DRINKABILITY: /10

DON'T DRINK AGAIN: **MIGHT ORDER AGAIN:** **GOING TO ORDER ANOTHER:**

LOCATION: **DATE:**

BEER NAME: **BEER STYLE:** **BREWERY:**

COLOUR:

CLARITY:
CLOUDY ☐☐☐☐☐☐☐☐☐☐ CRYSTAL

HEAD:
HEADLESS ☐☐☐☐☐☐☐☐☐☐ FLAKE?

HOP SCALE:

TASTE:
hoppy / malty / sweet / roasty / sour / other _____

AROMA:
hoppy / malty / fruity / floral / sour / other _____

NOTES: _____

AFTER TASTE: /10

DRINKABILITY: /10

DON'T DRINK AGAIN: 🌰 MIGHT ORDER AGAIN: 🌰 GOING TO ORDER ANOTHER: 🌰

LOCATION: **DATE:**

BEER NAME: **BEER STYLE:** **BREWERY:**

COLOUR:

CLARITY:
CLOUDY ☐☐☐☐☐☐☐☐☐☐ CRYSTAL

HEAD:
HEADLESS ☐☐☐☐☐☐☐☐☐☐ FLAKE?

HOP SCALE:

TASTE:
hoppy / malty / sweet / roasty / sour / other _____

AROMA:
hoppy / malty / fruity / floral / sour / other _____

NOTES: _____

AFTER TASTE: /10

DRINKABILITY: /10

DON'T DRINK AGAIN: 🌰 MIGHT ORDER AGAIN: 🌰 GOING TO ORDER ANOTHER: 🌰

LOCATION: **DATE:**

BEER NAME: **BEER STYLE:** **BREWERY:**

COLOUR:

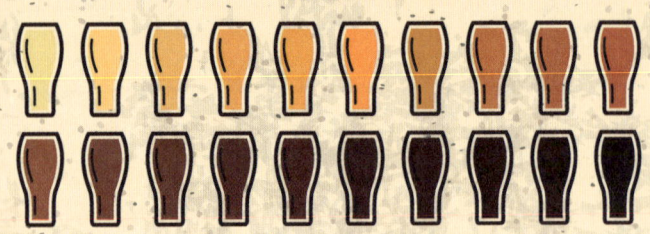

CLARITY:
CLOUDY ☐ ☐ ☐ ☐ ☐ ☐ ☐ ☐ ☐ ☐ CRYSTAL

HEAD:
HEADLESS ☐ ☐ ☐ ☐ ☐ ☐ ☐ ☐ ☐ ☐ FLAKE?

HOP SCALE:

TASTE:
hoppy / malty / sweet / roasty / sour / other _____

AROMA:
hoppy / malty / fruity / floral / sour / other _____

NOTES: _____

AFTER TASTE: /10

DRINKABILITY: /10

DON'T DRINK AGAIN: **MIGHT ORDER AGAIN:** **GOING TO ORDER ANOTHER:**

LOCATION: **DATE:**

BEER NAME: **BEER STYLE:** **BREWERY:**

COLOUR:

CLARITY:
CLOUDY ☐☐☐☐☐☐☐☐☐☐ CRYSTAL

HEAD:
HEADLESS ☐☐☐☐☐☐☐☐☐☐ FLAKE?

HOP SCALE:

TASTE:
hoppy / malty / sweet / roasty / sour / other _____

AROMA:
hoppy / malty / fruity / floral / sour / other _____

NOTES: _____

AFTER TASTE: /10

DRINKABILITY: /10

DON'T DRINK AGAIN: 🌰 MIGHT ORDER AGAIN: 🌰 GOING TO ORDER ANOTHER: 🌰

LOCATION:

DATE:

BEER NAME: **BEER STYLE:** **BREWERY:**

COLOUR:

CLARITY:

CLOUDY ☐☐☐☐☐☐☐☐☐☐ CRYSTAL

HEAD:

HEADLESS ☐☐☐☐☐☐☐☐☐☐ FLAKE?

HOP SCALE:

TASTE:

hoppy / malty / sweet / roasty / sour / other _____

AROMA:

hoppy / malty / fruity / floral / sour / other _____

NOTES: _____ **AFTER TASTE:** /10

_____ **DRINKABILITY:** /10

DON'T DRINK AGAIN: **MIGHT ORDER AGAIN:** **GOING TO ORDER ANOTHER:**

LOCATION:

DATE:

BEER NAME: **BEER STYLE:** **BREWERY:**

COLOUR:

CLARITY:

CLOUDY ▯▯▯▯▯▯▯▯▯▯ CRYSTAL

HEAD:

HEADLESS ▯▯▯▯▯▯▯▯▯▯ FLAKE?

HOP SCALE:

TASTE:

hoppy / malty / sweet / roasty / sour / other _____

AROMA:

hoppy / malty / fruity / floral / sour / other _____

NOTES: _____

AFTER TASTE: /10

DRINKABILITY: /10

DON'T DRINK AGAIN: 🍃 **MIGHT ORDER AGAIN:** 🍃 **GOING TO ORDER ANOTHER:** 🍃

YOU CAN USE BEER AS A CONDITIONER. THE PROTEINS AND VITAMINS IN BEER WILL HELP CLEANSE, SHINE AND SOFTEN YOUR DULL AND UNTIMELY LOCKS!

YOU CAN USE BEER TO SHINE UP ANY OLD COPPER ITEMS — OR REMOVE RUST FROM OLD BOLTS AND SCREWS!

FLAT BEER CAN BE WIPED OVER FURNITURE TO REVIVE COLOUR AND SHINE TO DULL AND OLD WOOD.

BEER CAN BE USED TO GET RID OF UNWANTED SLUGS AND SNAILS IN THE GARDEN. ADD TO A CONTAINER AND LEAVE OUTSIDE, SLUGS AND SNAILS WILL BE ATTRACTED TO THE SMELL AND BECOME TRAPPED WHEN LEANING IN FOR A SIP. YOU CAN USE THE SAME METHOD TO TRAP MICE, BUT REMEMBER NOT TO ADD TOO MUCH TO AVOID AN ACCIDENTAL DROWNING.

FOR ANY AVID BREAD MAKERS, ADDING BEER TO YOUR BREAD MIX MAKES FOR A FLAVOURSOME, HEARTY LOAF!

LOCATION: **DATE:**

BEER NAME: **BEER STYLE:** **BREWERY:**

COLOUR:

CLARITY:

CLOUDY ☐☐☐☐☐☐☐☐☐☐ CRYSTAL

HEAD:

HEADLESS ☐☐☐☐☐☐☐☐☐☐ FLAKE?

HOP SCALE:

TASTE:
hoppy / malty / sweet / roasty / sour / other _____

AROMA:
hoppy / malty / fruity / floral / sour / other _____

NOTES: _____

AFTER TASTE: /10

DRINKABILITY: /10

DON'T DRINK AGAIN: **MIGHT ORDER AGAIN:** **GOING TO ORDER ANOTHER:**

LOCATION: **DATE:**

BEER NAME: **BEER STYLE:** **BREWERY:**

COLOUR:

CLARITY:
CLOUDY ▢▢▢▢▢▢▢▢▢▢ CRYSTAL

HEAD:
HEADLESS ▢▢▢▢▢▢▢▢▢▢ FLAKE?

HOP SCALE:

TASTE:
hoppy / malty / sweet / roasty / sour / other _____

AROMA:
hoppy / malty / fruity / floral / sour / other _____

NOTES: _____

AFTER TASTE: /10

DRINKABILITY: /10

DON'T DRINK AGAIN 🍺 MIGHT ORDER AGAIN 🍺 GOING TO ORDER ANOTHER 🍺

LOCATION: **DATE:**

BEER NAME: **BEER STYLE:** **BREWERY:**

COLOUR:

CLARITY:

CLOUDY ☐☐☐☐☐☐☐☐☐☐ CRYSTAL

HEAD:

HEADLESS ☐☐☐☐☐☐☐☐☐☐ FLAKE?

HOP SCALE:

TASTE:
hoppy / malty / sweet / roasty / sour / other _____

AROMA:
hoppy / malty / fruity / floral / sour / other _____

NOTES: _____

AFTER TASTE: /10

DRINKABILITY: /10

DON'T DRINK AGAIN: ✿ **MIGHT ORDER AGAIN:** ✿ **GOING TO ORDER ANOTHER:** ✿

LOCATION: **DATE:**

BEER NAME: **BEER STYLE:** **BREWERY:**

COLOUR:

CLARITY:
CLOUDY ☐☐☐☐☐☐☐☐☐☐ CRYSTAL

HEAD:
HEADLESS ☐☐☐☐☐☐☐☐☐☐ FLAKE?

HOP SCALE:

TASTE:
hoppy / malty / sweet / roasty / sour / other _____

AROMA:
hoppy / malty / fruity / floral / sour / other _____

NOTES: _____

AFTER TASTE: /10

DRINKABILITY: /10

DON'T DRINK AGAIN 🌰   MIGHT ORDER AGAIN 🌰   GOING TO ORDER ANOTHER 🌰

LOCATION:

DATE:

BEER NAME: **BEER STYLE:** **BREWERY:**

COLOUR:

CLARITY:

CLOUDY ⬜⬜⬜⬜⬜⬜⬜⬜⬜⬜ CRYSTAL

HEAD:

HEADLESS ⬜⬜⬜⬜⬜⬜⬜⬜⬜⬜ FLAKE?

HOP SCALE:

TASTE:
hoppy / malty / sweet / roasty / sour / other _____

AROMA:
hoppy / malty / fruity / floral / sour / other _____

NOTES: _____

AFTER TASTE: /10

DRINKABILITY: /10

DON'T DRINK AGAIN: 🌰   MIGHT ORDER AGAIN: 🌰   GOING TO ORDER ANOTHER: 🌰

THE Best BEER IS AN Open BEER

LOCATION:

DATE:

BEER NAME: **BEER STYLE:**   **BREWERY:**

COLOUR:

CLARITY:
CLOUDY ▢▢▢▢▢▢▢▢▢▢ CRYSTAL

HEAD:
HEADLESS ▢▢▢▢▢▢▢▢▢▢ FLAKE?

HOP SCALE:

TASTE:
hoppy / malty / sweet / roasty / sour / other _____

AROMA:
hoppy / malty / fruity / floral / sour / other _____

NOTES: _____

AFTER TASTE: /10

DRINKABILITY: /10

DON'T DRINK AGAIN: **MIGHT ORDER AGAIN:**   **GOING TO ORDER ANOTHER:**

LOCATION: **DATE:**

BEER NAME: **BEER STYLE:**   **BREWERY:**

COLOUR:

CLARITY:
CLOUDY ☐☐☐☐☐☐☐☐☐☐ CRYSTAL

HEAD:
HEADLESS ☐☐☐☐☐☐☐☐☐☐ FLAKE?

HOP SCALE:

TASTE:
hoppy / malty / sweet / roasty / sour / other _____

AROMA:
hoppy / malty / fruity / floral / sour / other _____

NOTES: _____

AFTER TASTE: /10

DRINKABILITY: /10

DON'T DRINK AGAIN: **MIGHT ORDER AGAIN:**   **GOING TO ORDER ANOTHER:**

books by BOXER